Words **Joel Rickett**
Pictures **Spencer Wilson**

ModernABC.co.uk

is for Hummus

• A Modern Parent's ABC •

PENGUIN BOOKS

For Sophie, Esme, Gracie and Isla,
who finish all their hummus – sometimes.

Au pair

Aa

Aromatherapy

Aa

App

Bb

Balance bike

Baby carrier

Babyccino

Babyproofing

Blueberries

Baby genius

Baby yoga

Cc

Calpol

Carrot sticks

Catchment

Controlled crying

Dd

Drama

Dough balls

Equipped (for everything)

Electric toothbrush

Expecting

Ee

Eco-friendly

4x4

Ff

Face paint

Farrow & Ball

Glamping

Gg

Grobag

Growth spurt

Hummus

Hugh
(Fearnley-Whittingstall)

Hunter wellies

Hh

Helicopter
parenting

Kinaesthetic learning

Ketchup

Kk

Low-cost airline

Latching on

L l

Loft conversion

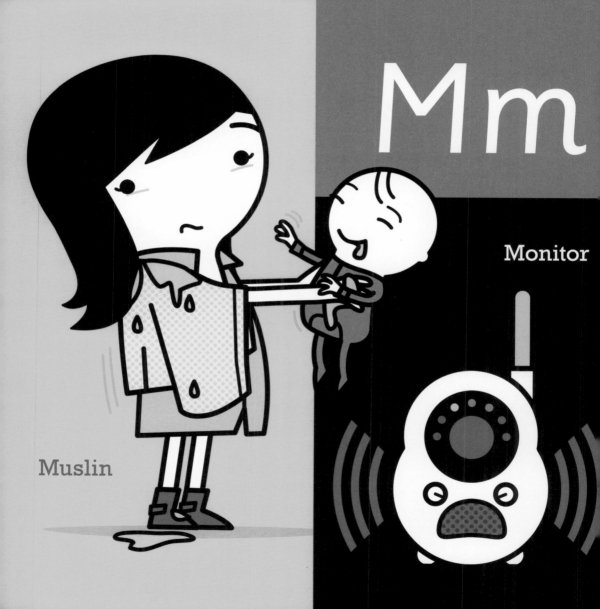

Mm

Muslin

Monitor

Nn

Naughty step

Nature
deficit
disorder

No!

Night feed

Ofsted
(outstanding)

Oo

Ocado

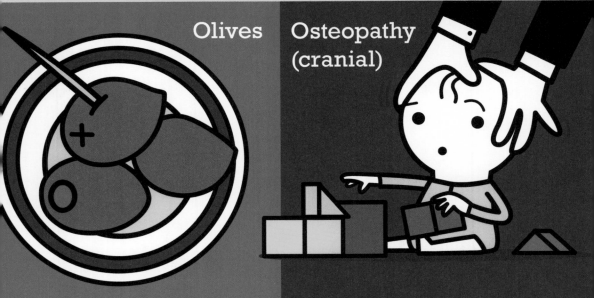

Olives

Osteopathy
(cranial)

Pp

Playdate

Projectile

Mush

Purée

Pump and dump

Qq

Regifting

TO: ~~Jack~~
Harry

Quinoa

Reward chart

Rr

Rhymetime

Rice cakes

Ss

Scooter (micro)

Swaddle

Squeezed middle

Soft play

Tt

Trunki

TENS machine

Unreasonable

Vaccination

Uu

Ultrasound

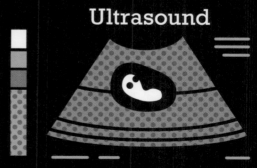

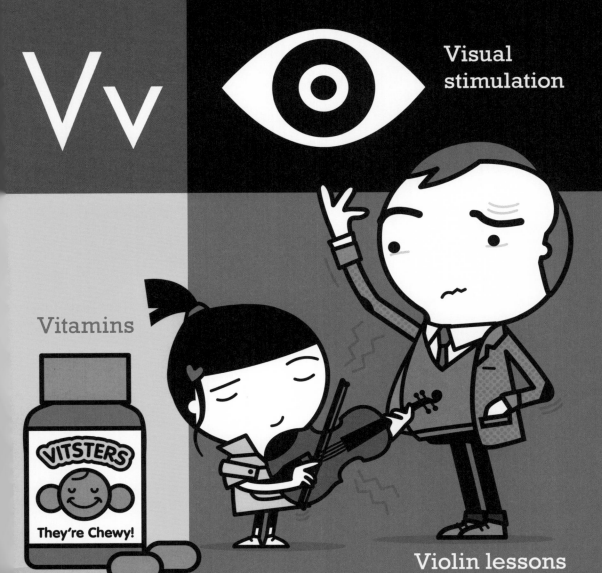

Ww

Wine time

Wheat intolerant

Yy

Yoghurt
(probiotic)

Yummy mummy

Joel Rickett

is a publisher and a (very) occasional writer.
His previous books include *How to Avoid Huge Ships* and *Whitstable Mum in Custard Shortage*. He lives in north London (of course), where he's a thoroughly modern parent to two gorgeous, demanding girls.

GONE
TO
LUNCH

Spencer Wilson

is an illustrator and co-founder of the illustration, design and animation company Peepshow Collective. He has been working to commission since 1998 in a world of coffee cups and ordered chaos; his work follows this theme with the creation of sketchy ideas and twisted thoughts. He lives in the modern parenting paradise that is Berkhamsted, Hertfordshire, with his wife and two girls, who never cease to inspire him.

www.spencerwilson.co.uk   www.peepshow.org.uk

VIKING

Published by the Penguin Group
Penguin Books Ltd, 80 Strand, London WC2R 0RL, England
Penguin Group (USA) Inc., 375 Hudson Street, New York, New York 10014, USA
Penguin Group (Canada), 90 Eglinton Avenue East, Suite 700, Toronto, Ontario, Canada M4P 2Y3
(a division of Pearson Penguin Canada Inc.)
Penguin Ireland, 25 St Stephen's Green, Dublin 2, Ireland (a division of Penguin Books Ltd)
Penguin Group (Australia), 707 Collins Street, Melbourne, Victoria 3008, Australia
(a division of Pearson Australia Group Pty Ltd)
Penguin Books India Pvt Ltd, 11 Community Centre,
Panchsheel Park, New Delhi – 110 017, India
Penguin Group (NZ), 67 Apollo Drive, Rosedale, Auckland 0632, New Zealand
(a division of Pearson New Zealand Ltd)
Penguin Books (South Africa) (Pty) Ltd, Block D, Rosebank Office Park,
181 Jan Smuts Avenue, Parktown North, Gauteng 2193, South Africa

Penguin Books Ltd, Registered Offices: 80 Strand, London WC2R 0RL, England

www.penguin.com

First published 2013
001

Set in Rockwell, Sasson and Frutiger
Designed by Spencer Wilson
Printed in China

A CIP catalogue record for this book is available from the British Library

ISBN: 978–0–670–92253–6

a b c d e f
o p q